quick and healthy
low-fat pasta

Consultant Editor:
Valerie Ferguson

HERMES
HOUSE

Contents

Introduction

Some fat in the diet is essential, but too much can be damaging and nutritionists recommend that most people should reduce their intake, particularly of saturated fats. Pasta is perfect food, as it contains very little fat, but is high in complex carbohydrates, which provide a steady release of energy, and which, it is recommended, should form half of our daily diets.

Pasta is immensely versatile and combines superbly with many low-fat ingredients, including vegetables, fish and seafood, poultry and lean meat, as well as herbs and spices. It is perfect for all kinds of dishes, from light lunches to family suppers.

All of the mouth-watering recipes in this book have nutritional notes, giving the total fat, saturated fat, cholesterol, fibre content and energy value per portion. This at-a-glance information makes meal planning simplicity itself.

Pasta is always a family favourite, whether fresh or dried, in ribbons or chunky shapes, baked in layers or filled and served with a luscious sauce. Most of these recipes are quick and easy, and most contain less than 14 g total fat per portion. They are all absolutely delicious, so you and your family can enjoy satisfying meals and look after your health as well.

Types of Pasta

There are at least 200 different types of pasta – and there can sometimes seem to be about ten times as many names.

Most pasta is made from durum wheat flour, which is quite hard and does not go soggy when cooked. Dried pasta may simply have been mixed with water or may also contain egg, while fresh pasta – *pasta all'uova* – always contains egg. As a result of a growing interest in healthy foods, whole wheat pasta, which has a rich brown colour, has become increasingly popular. Buckwheat pasta, which is an even darker colour, is also available and is suitable for people on a gluten-free diet. Pasta may be coloured and flavoured with a range of ingredients. The most common additions are tomatoes and spinach, but beetroot, saffron, herbs, wild mushrooms and cuttlefish ink are also widely used.

There are no hard-and-fast rules about which shapes to serve with particular sauces, but some shapes do work better than others. The recipes in this book include a recommendation, but you can substitute a shape of your choice.

Above: A selection from the huge range of different kinds of pasta

Hollow Pasta

These include penne, fusilli, macaroni, farfalle, rigatoni, orecchiette, rotelli, tortiglioni, chifferi rigati, ruote and mezze. Try these with robust sauces, such as cheese, tomato and vegetable.

Long Pasta

These include spaghetti, linguine, tagliatelle, tagliarini and fettuccine. Some are flat ribbons, while others are hollow tubes. All go well with smooth and creamy sauces and vegetable sauce with finely chopped ingredients.

Filled Pasta

These include ravioli, cappelletti and tortelloni. These are good with simple sauces, such as tomato.

Pasta for Baking

These include very delicate shapes, such as risi and orzi, as well as larger ones for more robust dishes – tubetti conchiglie, cannelloni and lasagne, for example.

Basic Pasta Dough

Serves 3–4

INGREDIENTS
200 g/7 oz/1¾ cups plain flour,
(Italian tipo 00 is the best if you
can find it)
pinch of salt
2 eggs
10 ml/2 tsp cold water

Making Pasta by Hand

1 Sift the flour and salt on to a clean work surface and make a well in the centre with your hand.

2 Put the eggs and water into the well. Using a fork, beat the eggs gently together, then gradually draw in the flour from the sides, combining to make a thick pasta.

3 When the mixture becomes too stiff to use a fork, use your hands to continue to combine to form a firm dough. Knead the dough for about 5 minutes, until it is smooth.

4 Wrap the dough in clear film and leave it to rest for 20–30 minutes.

Making Pasta in a Food Processor

1 Sift the flour into the bowl of the food processor and add a pinch of salt.

2 Beat the eggs with the water and pour into the flour. Process the mixture until the dough begins to come together. Tip it out and knead until smooth. Wrap in clear film and leave to rest for 30 minutes.

VARIATIONS: Tomato: add 20 ml/4 tsp concentrated tomato purée to the eggs before mixing.
Spinach: add 115 g/4 oz frozen spinach, thawed and squeezed of excess moisture. Combine or process with the eggs, before adding the mixture to the flour.
Herb: add 45 ml/3 tbsp finely chopped fresh herbs to the eggs before mixing the dough.
Wholemeal: use 50 g/2 oz plain flour and 150 g/5 oz wholemeal flour. Add an extra 10 ml/2 tsp cold water.

Fat & Calorie Counter

The following figures show the weight of fat (g) and the energy content per 90 g/3½ oz of each food. Use them to plan your meals, remembering to allow for any cooking fats or dressings.

Vegetables	Fat (g)	Energy
Artichokes, globe, boiled	0.2	24 Kcal/101 kJ
Asparagus, boiled	0.6	25 Kcal/103 kj
Aubergines, raw	0.4	15 Kcal/64 kJ
Broccoli, raw	0.9	33 Kcal/138 kJ
Carrots, raw	0.9	35 Kcal/146 kJ
Celery, raw	0.2	7 Kcal/29 kJ
Courgettes, raw	0.4	18 Kcal/74 kJ
Fennel, Florence, raw	0.2	12 Kcal/50 kJ
Mushrooms, raw	0.4	13 Kcal/55 kJ
Olives, in brine	11.0	103 Kcal/422 kJ
Onions, raw	0.2	36 Kcal/150 kJ
Peas, raw	1.5	83 Kcal/344 kJ
Peppers, red, raw	0.4	32 Kcal/134 kJ
Spinach, raw	0.8	25 Kcal/103 kJ
Tomatoes, raw	0.3	17 Kcal/73 kJ

Fruit & Nuts	Fat (g)	Energy
Apples, eating, raw	0.1	47 Kcal/199 kJ
Oranges	0.1	37 Kcal/158 kJ
Pine nuts	68.6	688 Kcal/2840 kJ
Raisins	0.4	272 Kcal/1159 kJ
Walnuts	68.5	688 Kcal/2840 kJ

Pasta	Fat (g)	Energy
Pasta, white, cooked	0.7	104 Kcal/437 kJ
Pasta, wholemeal, cooked	0.9	113 Kcal/475 kJ

Beans & Pulses	Fat (g)	Energy
Green and brown lentils, cooked	0.7	105 Kcal/446 kJ
Red kidney beans, canned	0.6	100 Kcal/424 kJ

Fish & Shellfish	Fat (g)	Energy
Anchovies, canned in oil	19.9	280 Kcal/1165 kJ
Clams, canned in natural juice	0.6	77 Kcal/325 kJ
Crab, canned in brine	0.5	77 Kcal/325 kJ
Prawns, boiled	0.9	99 Kcal/418 kJ
Salmon, raw	11	180 Kcal/750 kJ
Salmon, smoked	4.5	142 Kcal/598 kJ
Salmon, steamed	11.9	194 Kcal/812 kJ
Scallops, queen, steamed	1.4	118 Kcal/496 kJ
Squid, raw	1.7	81 Kcal/344 kJ
Tuna, canned in brine	0.6	99 Kcal/422 kJ

Meat & Poultry	Fat (g)	Energy
Bacon rashers, lean back, grilled	5.2	172 Kcal/722 kJ
Beef mince, extra lean, stewed	6.6	121 Kcal/508 kJ
Beef, topside, lean, roast	4.4	156 Kcal/655 kJ
Chicken breast, no skin, roast	1.1	153 Kcal/643 kJ
Duck, meat only, roast	10.4	195 Kcal/819 kJ
Lamb, leg, lean, roast	9.6	210 Kcal/822 kJ
Pork, leg, lean, roast	6.9	185 Kcal/777 kJ
Turkey, meat only, roast	2.0	153 Kcal/643 kJ

Dairy, Fats & Oils	Fat (g)	Energy
Butter	81.7	737 Kcal/3031 kJ
Cream cheese	47.4	439 Kcal/1807 kJ
Curd cheese	11.7	173 Kcal/723 kJ
Eggs, whole, raw	10.8	147 Kcal/612 kJ
Egg white, raw	Trace	36 Kcal/153 kJ
Egg yolk, raw	30.5	339 Kcal/1402 kJ
Fromage frais, plain	7.1	113 Kcal/469 kJ
Fromage frais, very low-fat	0.2	58 Kcal/247 kJ
Low-fat cottage cheese	1.4	78 Kcal/324 kJ
Low-fat crème fraîche	15.0	165 Kcal/683 kJ
Low-fat soft cheese	Trace	74 Kcal/313 kJ
Low-fat spread	40.5	39 Kcal/1605 kJ
Low-fat yogurt, natural	0.8	56 Kcal/236 kJ
Margarine	81.6	739 Kcal/3039 kJ
Mayonnaise, reduced-fat	28.1	288 Kcal/1188 kJ
Milk, skimmed	0.1	33 Kcal/140 kJ
Olive oil	99.9	899 Kcal/3696 kJ
Parmesan cheese	32.7	452 Kcal/1880 kJ
Very low-fat spread	25.0	273 Kcal/1128 kJ

Information from *The Composition of Foods* (5th Edition, 1991) is Crown copyright and is reproduced with the permission of the Royal Society of Chemistry and the Controller of Her Majesty's Stationery Office.

Low-fat Substitutes

There are plenty of alternatives to high-fat ingredients to choose from. Be sure to eat a good variety of different foods every day to make sure you get all the nutrients you need.

Dairy Products

Replace whole milk with skimmed or semi-skimmed milk, which have the same amount of protein, calcium and B vitamins. Use low-fat yogurt or low-fat crème fraîche instead of cream, soured cream or full-fat yogurt. If you strain low-fat yogurt through muslin, it will become as thick as crème fraîche. Substitute reduced-fat cheese for hard cheeses, such as Parmesan; it has about half the fat content. Low-fat soft cheeses are widely available.

Meat & Poultry

Red meats are high in saturated fats so eat them sparingly. Buy extra lean cuts and trim off all visible fat. Remove the skin and any visible fat from poultry before cooking. Eating a vegetarian dish at least once a week is another painless way to reduce your intake of saturated fats from meat. With the influence of the Mediterranean diet there are many tasty options available. For example, pulses, such as lentils and dried beans, are a very useful source of protein, and fish and seafood are also good alternatives to meat. Even oily fish, such as tuna and salmon, are lower in fat than chicken, and the fat they do contain is unsaturated.

Above: A selection of oils that are low in saturates and low-fat spread.

Fats & Oils

Butter is high in saturated fats and so are some margarines. Use low-fat or very low-fat spreads wherever possible, but remember that these products are not always suitable for cooking. Instead, where possible use oils that are low in saturated fats, such as olive oil, which has an excellent and authentically Italian flavour. You can keep the amount of oil required to a minimum by using non-stick or heavy-based pans. Using an oil in a spray container enables you to control how much you are using.

Clam & Pasta Soup

This recipe uses store-cupboard ingredients to create a delicious and filling low-fat soup. Serve it with hot focaccia for an informal supper.

Serves 4

INGREDIENTS
15 ml/1 tbsp olive oil
1 large onion, finely chopped
2 garlic cloves, crushed
400 g/14 oz can chopped tomatoes
15 ml/1 tbsp sun-dried
   tomato purée
5 ml/1 tsp sugar
5 ml/1 tsp dried mixed Italian herbs
about 750 ml/1¼ pints/3 cups fish or
   vegetable stock, plus extra if required
150 ml/¼ pint/⅔ cup red wine
50 g/2 oz/½ cup small dried
   pasta shapes
150 g/5 oz jar or can clams in
   natural juice
30 ml/2 tbsp finely chopped fresh flat leaf
   parsley, plus a few whole leaves
   to garnish
salt and freshly ground black pepper

1 Heat the oil in a large saucepan. Cook the onion gently, stirring frequently for 5 minutes, until softened and translucent.

Nutritional Notes	
Energy	165 Kcal/695 kJ
Total fat	3.4 g
Saturated fat	0.4 g
Cholesterol	0 mg
Fibre	1.5 g

2 Add the crushed garlic, chopped tomatoes, tomato purèe, sugar, mixed herbs, fish or vegetable stock and wine and season with salt and freshly ground black pepper to taste. Bring the mixture to the boil. Reduce the heat, half cover the pan and simmer for 10 minutes, stirring occasionally.

3 Add the pasta shapes to the pan, stir well and bring back to the boil. Allow the mixture to simmer uncovered for 10 minutes, or until the pasta is *al dente*.

4 Add the clams and their juice and heat through for 3–4 minutes, adding more stock if required. Do not let it boil or the clams will become tough. Remove from the heat, stir in the chopped parsley and adjust the seasoning. Serve hot, ladled into soup bowls and sprinkled with pepper and parsley leaves to garnish.

Little Stuffed Hats in Broth

This is served in northern Italy on St. Stephen's Day and at New Year.

Serves 4

INGREDIENTS

1.2 litres/2 pints/5 cups chicken stock
90–115 g/3½–4 oz/1 cup fresh or
   dried cappelletti
30 ml/2 tbsp dry white wine (optional)
15 ml/1 tbsp finely chopped fresh flat leaf
   parsley (optional)
salt and freshly ground black pepper
shredded flat leaf parsley, to garnish
15 ml/1 tbsp freshly grated Parmesan
   cheese, to serve

1 Pour the chicken stock into a large saucepan and bring to the boil. Season to taste. Add the pasta, stir well and return to the boil. Reduce the heat and simmer until the pasta is *al dente*.

2 Swirl in the wine and parsley, if using, then adjust the seasoning. Ladle into warmed soup bowls, then sprinkle with shredded flat leaf parsley and grated Parmesan. Serve immediately.

Nutritional Notes	
Energy	103 Kcal/436 kJ
Total fat	1.7 g
Saturated fat	0.8 g
Cholesterol	3.7 mg
Fibre	0.8 g

Tiny Pasta in Broth

In Italy, this tasty soup is often served with bread for a quick snack.

Serves 4

INGREDIENTS

1.2 litres/2 pints/5 cups beef stock
75 g/3 oz/¾ cup dried tiny soup pasta,
   such as funghetti
2 pieces bottled roasted red pepper,
   about 50 g/2 oz, drained and diced
salt and freshly ground
   black pepper
25 g/1 oz coarsely shaved Parmesan cheese,
   to serve

1 Bring the beef stock to the boil in a large saucepan. Season, then add the pasta. Stir well and return to the boil. Reduce the heat and simmer for 7–8 minutes, until the pasta is *al dente*.

2 Place the red pepper in four soup bowls. Check the soup for seasoning, then serve in the bowls, with shaved Parmesan offered separately.

Nutritional Notes	
Energy	108 Kcal/457 kJ
Total fat	3.7 g
Saturated fat	1.5 g
Cholesterol	6.2 mg
Fibre	0.8 g

Right: Little Stuffed Hats in Broth (top); Tiny Pasta in Broth

Roasted Tomato & Pasta Soup

When the only tomatoes you can buy are not particularly flavoursome,
make this soup. The oven-roasting compensates for any lack of flavour.

Serves 4

INGREDIENTS
450 g/1 lb ripe Italian plum tomatoes
    halved lengthways
1 large red pepper, quartered lengthways
    and deseeded
1 large red onion, quartered lengthways
2 garlic cloves, unpeeled
15 ml/1 tbsp olive oil
1.2 litres/2 pints/5 cups vegetable stock
    or water
pinch of sugar
90 g/3½ oz/scant 1 cup dried small pasta
    shapes, such as tubetti or small macaroni
salt and freshly ground black pepper
fresh basil leaves, to garnish

1 Preheat the oven to 190°C/375°F/
Gas 5. Spread out the tomatoes, red
pepper, onion and garlic in a roasting
tin and drizzle with the olive oil.
Roast for 30–40 minutes, until the
vegetables are soft and charred, stirring
and turning them halfway through the
cooking time.

2 Tip the roasted vegetables into a
blender or food processor, add about
250 ml/8 fl oz/1 cup of the vegetable
stock or water and process the mixture
until puréed.

3 Scrape into a sieve placed over a
large saucepan and press the purée
through the sieve into the pan. Discard
the contents of the sieve.

4 Add the remaining stock or water,
add the sugar and season with salt and
freshly ground black pepper to taste.
Bring to the boil, stirring.

Nutritional Notes	
Energy	145 Kcal/611 kJ
Total fat	4.6 g
Saturated fat	0.7 g
Cholesterol	0 mg
Fibre	2.4 g

Add the pasta, stir well and bring back to the boil. Simmer, stirring frequently, for 4–5 minutes, or until the pasta is *al dente*. Adjust the seasoning. Serve hot in bowls, with fresh basil leaves and black pepper.

COOK'S TIP: For extra convenience, the soup can be frozen without the pasta. Allow to thaw and then bring to the boil before adding the pasta shapes.

Lentil & Pasta Soup

Serves 6

INGREDIENTS

175 g/6 oz/¾ cup brown lentils
3 garlic cloves
1 litre/1¾ pint/4 cups water
15 ml/1 tbsp olive oil
1 onion, finely chopped
2 celery sticks, finely chopped
30 ml/2 tbsp sun-dried tomato purée
1.75 litres/3 pints/7½ cups vegetable stock
fresh marjoram, basil and
    thyme leaves
50 g/2 oz/½ cup dried small pasta shapes,
    such as tubetti
salt and freshly ground black pepper
tiny fresh herb leaves, to garnish

1 Put the lentils in a large saucepan with the water and one lightly smashed, unpeeled garlic clove. Bring to the boil, then lower the heat and simmer, stirring occasionally, for about 20 minutes or until tender. Rinse in a sieve, reserving the garlic, and drain.

2 Heat the oil in a large saucepan. Cook the chopped onion and celery over a low heat, stirring frequently, for 5–7 minutes, until softened.

3 Crush the remaining garlic, then peel and mash the reserved garlic. Add to the vegetables with the tomato purée and lentils. Stir, pour in the stock, then add herbs and seasoning to taste. Bring to the boil, then simmer for 30 minutes, stirring occasionally.

4 Add the pasta, stir and return to the boil. Simmer for 7–8 minutes until the pasta is *al dente*. Serve hot, sprinkled with the herb leaves.

Nutritional Notes	
Energy	145 Kcal/615 kJ
Total fat	3.2 g
Saturated fat	0.4 g
Cholesterol	0 g
Fibre	3.2 g

Farmhouse Soup

Serves 6

INGREDIENTS

15 ml/1 tbsp olive oil
1 onion, roughly chopped
3 carrots, cut into large chunks
175–200 g/6–7 oz turnips, cut
   into chunks
175 g/6 oz swede, cut into large chunks
400 g/14 oz can chopped Italian tomatoes
15 ml/1 tbsp tomato purée
5 ml/1 tsp dried mixed herbs
5 ml/1 tsp dried oregano
50 g/2 oz/½ cup dried peppers, washed and
   thinly sliced (optional)
1.5 litres/2½ pints/6¼ cups
   vegetable stock
50 g/2 oz/½ cup dried small macaroni
   or conchiglie
400 g/14 oz can red kidney beans, rinsed
   and drained
30 ml/2 tbsp chopped fresh
   flat leaf parsley
salt and freshly ground black pepper
15 ml/1 tbsp freshly grated Parmesan cheese,
   to serve

1 Heat the oil in a large saucepan, add the onion and cook over a low heat, stirring occasionally for about 5 minutes, until softened. Add the fresh vegetables, tomatoes, tomato purée, dried herbs and dried peppers, if using. Season to taste. Pour in the stock and bring to the boil. Stir well, cover, reduce the heat and simmer for 30 minutes, stirring occasionally.

2 Add the pasta, stir well and return to the boil. Simmer, uncovered, for about 5 minutes, until the pasta is *al dente*.

3 Add the beans. Heat through, then add the parsley. Check the seasoning. Serve hot, sprinkled with Parmesan.

Nutritional Notes	
Energy	159 Kcal/671 kJ
Total fat	4.0 g
Saturated fat	0.9 g
Cholesterol	2.36 mg
Fibre	6.6 g

Farfalle with Tuna

This is a quick and simple dish that makes a good low-fat weekday supper if you have canned tomatoes and tuna in the store cupboard.

Serves 4

INGREDIENTS
15 ml/1 tbsp olive oil
1 small onion, finely chopped
1 garlic clove, finely chopped
400 g/14 oz can chopped Italian
    plum tomatoes
45 ml/3 tbsp dry white wine
8–10 stoned black olives, sliced
    into rings
10 ml/2 tsp chopped fresh oregano
    or 5 ml/1 tsp dried oregano, plus
    extra fresh oregano to garnish
350 g/12 oz/3 cups dried farfalle
175 g/6 oz can tuna in brine
salt and freshly ground
    black pepper

1 Heat the olive oil in a medium frying pan or saucepan, and add the onion and garlic. Cook gently, stirring occasionally, for 2–3 minutes, until the onion is soft and golden.

Nutritional Notes	
Energy	387 Kcal/1643 kJ
Total fat	4.9 g
Saturated fat	0.8 g
Cholesterol	21.3 mg
Fibre	3.5 g

2 Add the tomatoes and bring to the boil, then add the wine and simmer for 1–2 minutes. Stir in the sliced black olives and the fresh or dried oregano and season with salt and pepper to taste. Cover and cook, stirring occasionally, for 20–25 minutes.

3 Meanwhile, cook the pasta in a large saucepan of lightly salted boiling water until it is *al dente*.

4 Drain the canned tuna and flake it with a fork. Add to the tomato sauce with about 60 ml/4 tbsp of the pasta water and stir to mix. Adjust the seasoning to taste.

5 Drain the pasta and tip it into a warmed serving bowl. Pour the sauce over the top and toss to mix. Serve immediately, garnished with oregano.

VARIATION: If you like capers, try adding a few to the sauce in place of some of the olives.

Penne with Salmon & Dill

Although an oily fish, salmon is a healthy choice because it contains essential, cholesterol-lowering fatty acids.

Serves 6

INGREDIENTS
350 g/12 oz salmon fillet, skinned
115 g/4 oz sliced smoked salmon
1–2 shallots, finely chopped
115 g/4 oz button mushrooms, quartered
150 ml/¼ pint/⅔ cup light red or rosé wine
150 ml/¼ pint/⅔ cup fish stock
150 ml/¼ pint/⅔ cup low-fat crème fraîche
30 ml/2 tbsp chopped fresh dill
350 g/12 oz/3 cups penne
salt and freshly ground black pepper
fresh dill sprigs, to garnish

2 Put the shallots and mushrooms into a pan with the wine. Bring to the boil and cook for about 5 minutes, or until the juices are almost reduced.

3 Add the fish stock and crème fraîche and stir until smooth. Then add the fresh salmon, cover the pan and simmer gently for 2–3 minutes. Remove from the heat and stir in the chopped dill and seasoning.

1 Cut the fresh salmon into 2.5 cm/1 in cubes. Cut the smoked salmon into 1 cm/½ in strips.

Nutritional Notes	
Energy	394 Kcal/1656 kJ
Total fat	12.8 g
Saturated fat	4.6 g
Cholesterol	64 mg
Fibre	2.0 g

COOK'S TIP: You might like to make the sauce in a non-stick saucepan to prevent any difficulties when you leave it to simmer.

4 Meanwhile, cook the pasta in a large saucepan of lightly salted boiling water, until it is *al dente*. Drain and transfer to a warmed serving dish. Add the smoked salmon to the sauce and pour over the pasta. Toss lightly to mix. Serve at once, garnished with sprigs of dill.

21

Spaghetti with Clam Sauce

This is probably one of Italy's most famous pasta dishes, and is sometimes translated as "white clam sauce", in order to distinguish it from that other classic recipe, clams in tomato sauce.

Serves 4

INGREDIENTS

1 kg/2¼ lb fresh clams
15 ml/1 tbsp olive oil
45 ml/3 tbsp chopped fresh
    flat leaf parsley
120 ml/4 fl oz/½ cup dry
    white wine
275 g/10 oz dried spaghetti
2 garlic cloves
salt and freshly ground black pepper

1 Scrub the clams under cold running water, discarding any that are open or that do not close when sharply tapped against the work surface.

2 Heat half the oil in a large saucepan, add the clams and 15 ml/ 1 tbsp of the parsley and cook over a high heat for a few seconds. Pour in the white wine, then cover tightly. Cook for about 5 minutes, shaking the pan frequently, until the clams have opened.

Nutritional Notes	
Energy	425 Kcal/1789 kJ
Total fat	4.5 g
Saturated fat	0.4 g
Cholesterol	0 mg
Fibre	1.5 g

3 Meanwhile, cook the pasta in a large saucepan of lightly salted boiling water, until it is *al dente*.

4 Using a slotted spoon, transfer the clams to a bowl, discarding any that have failed to open. Strain the cooking liquid and set it aside. Put eight clams to one side, then remove the rest from their shells.

5 Heat the remaining oil in a clean saucepan. Cook the whole garlic cloves over a medium heat until golden, crushing them with the back of a spoon. Remove the garlic.

Add the shelled clams to the pan, gradually add 150 ml/¼ pint/⅔ cup of the reserved liquid, than add pepper. Cook for 1–2 minutes, adding more liquid as the sauce reduces. Add the remaining parsley and cook, stirring occasionally, for 1–2 minutes.

7 Drain the pasta, add it to the pan and toss. Serve in dishes, scooping the shelled clams from the bottom of the pan and placing some of them on top of each serving. Garnish with the reserved clams in their shells, parsley and pepper and serve immediately.

Linguine with Crab

This Roman dish is perfect for a tasty family lunch or supper accompanied by crusty Italian bread.

Serves 4

INGREDIENTS
250 g/9 oz shelled white crab meat
15 ml/1 tbsp olive oil
1 small handful of fresh flat leaf parsley,
   roughly chopped, plus extra
   to garnish
1 garlic clove, crushed
350 g/12 oz ripe Italian plum tomatoes,
   peeled and chopped
60–90 ml/4–6 tbsp dry white wine
350 g/12 oz dried linguine
salt and freshly ground black pepper

1 Put the crab meat in a mortar and pound to a rough pulp with a pestle, or use a sturdy bowl and the end of a rolling pin. Set aside.

COOK'S TIP: Ask a fishmonger to remove crab meat from the shells, or buy dressed crab at the supermarket. Alternatively, use drained canned crab meat.

2 Heat the oil in a large saucepan. Add the parsley and garlic, season to taste, and cook until the garlic begins to brown, stirring occasionally.

3 Stir in the tomatoes, pounded crab meat and wine, cover the pan, bring to the boil, then reduce the heat and simmer the mixture for 15 minutes, stirring occasionally.

4 Meanwhile, cook the pasta in a large saucepan of lightly salted boiling water until it is *al dente*. Drain, reserving a little of the cooking water Return the pasta to the clean pan.

Nutritional Notes	
Energy	308 Kcal/1307 kJ
Total fat	5 g
Saturated fat	0.7 g
Cholesterol	32.1 mg
Fibre	2.3 g

5 Add the tomato and crab mixture to the pasta and toss to mix, adding a little cooking water if necessary. Adjust the seasoning to taste. Serve hot, in warmed bowls, sprinkled with the extra chopped parsley.

Tagliatelle with Scallops

Serves 4

INGREDIENTS
200 g/7 oz fresh scallops, sliced
30 ml/2 tbsp plain flour
15 ml/1 tbsp olive oil
2 spring onions, cut into rings
½–1 small fresh red chilli, seeded and very
  finely chopped
15 ml/1 tbsp finely chopped flat leaf parsley,
  plus extra to garnish
60 ml/4 tbsp brandy
105 ml/7 tbsp fish stock
275 g/10 oz fresh spinach-flavoured tagliatelle
salt and freshly ground black pepper

1 Toss the scallops in the flour. Heat the oil in a frying pan. Add the spring onions, chilli and parsley. Cook over a medium heat, stirring, for 1–2 minutes. Add the scallops and toss for another 1–2 minutes.

2 Pour over the brandy. Set alight. When died down, add the stock, season and stir. Simmer briefly, then cover and remove from the heat. Meanwhile cook the pasta, add to the sauce and serve.

Nutritional Notes	
Energy	372 Kcal/1570 kJ
Total fat	4.8 g
Saturated fat	0.7 g
Cholesterol	0 mg
Fibre	2.2 g

Spaghetti with Squid & Peas

Serves 4

INGREDIENTS
450 g/1 lb prepared squid
10 ml/2 tsp olive oil
1 small onion, finely chopped
400 g/14 oz can chopped Italian plum tomatoes
1 garlic clove, finely chopped
15 ml/1 tbsp red wine vinegar
5 ml/1 tsp sugar
10 ml/2 tsp finely chopped fresh rosemary
115 g/4 oz/1 cup frozen peas
275 g/10 oz dried spaghetti
15 ml/1 tbsp chopped fresh flat leaf parsley
salt and freshly ground black pepper

1 Cut the squid into strips, chopping any tentacles. Set aside. Fry the onion in the oil until softened. Stir in the squid, tomatoes, garlic, vinegar and sugar.

2 Add the rosemary and seasoning. Bring to the boil, then cover and simmer, stirring occasionally, for 20 minutes. Add the peas and cook for 10 minutes. Cook the pasta in lightly salted boiling water until al dente. Drain and serve with the sauce and parsley.

Nutritional Notes	
Energy	285 Kcal/1206 kJ
Total fat	4 g
Saturated fat	0.4 g
Cholesterol	0 mg
Fibre	3 g

Spinach Tagliarini with Chicken & Asparagus

This is an unusual and delicate pasta dish and would be the perfect choice for a healthy summer lunch.

Serves 4–6

INGREDIENTS

2 skinless, boneless chicken breasts
15 ml/1 tbsp light soy sauce
30 ml/2 tbsp sherry
30 ml/2 tbsp cornflour
8 spring onions, cut into 2.5 cm/1 in
    diagonal slices
1–2 garlic cloves, crushed
needle shreds of rind of ½ lemon and
    30 ml/2 tbsp lemon juice
150 ml/¼ pint/⅔ cup
    chicken stock
5 ml/1 tsp caster sugar
225 g/8 oz slender asparagus spears,
    cut into 7.5 cm/3 in lengths
450 g/1 lb fresh tagliarini pasta
salt and freshly ground
    black pepper

1 Place the chicken breasts between two sheets of clear film and flatten them to a thickness of about 5 mm/ ¼ in with a rolling-pin.

Nutritional Notes	
Energy	369 Kcal/1548 kJ
Total fat	6.9 g
Saturated fat	1.8 g
Cholesterol	142 mg
Fibre	3.4 g

2 Cut the chicken into 2.5 cm/1 in strips across the grain of the fillets. Put the chicken into a bowl with the soy sauce, sherry, cornflour, salt and freshly ground black pepper. Toss to coat.

3 Put the chicken, spring onions, garlic and shreds of lemon rind into a large non-stick pan. Add the chicken stock and bring to the boil, stirring constantly until thickened. Add the sugar, lemon juice and asparagus pieces. Simmer the sauce for 4–5 minutes, until the chicken and asparagus are tender.

4 Meanwhile, cook the pasta in a large saucepan of lightly salted boiling water until it is *al dente*. Drain, arrange on warmed serving plates and spoon over the chicken and asparagus sauce. Serve immediately.

Spaghetti alla Carbonara

This is a low-fat variation of the classic Italian dish, using lean smoked back bacon rashers and low-fat cream cheese.

Serves 4

INGREDIENTS

150 g/5 oz lean smoked back
   bacon rashers
1 onion, chopped
1–2 garlic cloves, crushed
150 ml/¼ pint/⅔ cup chicken stock
150 ml/¼ pint/⅔ cup dry
   white wine
200 g/7 oz low-fat soft cheese
450 g/1 lb chilli and garlic-flavoured
   dried spaghetti
30 ml/2 tbsp chopped fresh parsley
salt and freshly ground
   black pepper
Parmesan cheese, to serve

2 Add the wine and boil rapidly unt reduced by half. Whisk in the cheese and season to taste with salt and fresh ground black pepper.

3 Meanwhile, cook the spaghetti in large saucepan of lightly salted boilin water until it is *al dente*.

1 Cut the bacon rashers into 1 cm/½ in strips. Fry quickly in a non-stick frying pan for 2–3 minutes, stirring. Add the onion, garlic and stock to the pan. Bring to the boil, cover, then reduce the heat and simmer for about 5 minutes, until the bacon and onion are tender.

Nutritional Notes	
Energy	428 Kcal/1815 kJ
Total fat	4.6 g
Saturated fat	1.6 g
Cholesterol	9.96 mg
Fibre	3.0 g

4 Drain and return the cooked spaghetti to the pan with the sauce and parsley, toss well and serve immediately topped with a few thin shavings of Parmesan cheese.

Rigatoni with Pork

This is an excellent and very tasty, low-fat meat sauce made using minced pork rather than the more usual minced beef.

Serves 4

INGREDIENTS

15 ml/1 tbsp olive oil
1 small onion, finely chopped
½ carrot, finely chopped
½ celery stick, finely chopped
2 garlic cloves, finely chopped
150 g/5 oz extra-lean
    minced pork
60 ml/4 tbsp dry white wine
400 g/14 oz can chopped Italian
    plum tomatoes
a few fresh basil leaves, plus extra
    to garnish
400 g/14 oz/3½ cups dried rigatoni
salt and freshly ground
    black pepper
shaved Parmesan cheese,
    to serve (optional)

1 Heat the oil in a large frying pan or saucepan until just sizzling, add the onion, carrot, celery and garlic and cook over a medium heat, stirring frequently, for 3–4 minutes.

2 Add the minced pork and cook gently for 2–3 minutes, breaking up any lumps with a wooden spoon.

3 Reduce the heat and cook for a further 2–3 minutes, stirring frequently, then stir in the wine. Mix in the tomatoes, basil leaves and salt and pepper to taste. Bring to the boil, then reduce the heat, cover and simmer for 40 minutes, stirring occasionally.

4 Cook the pasta in a large saucepan of lightly salted boiling water until it *al dente.* Just before draining it, add a ladleful or two of the cooking water to the sauce. Stir well, then taste the sauce and adjust the seasoning.

Nutritional Notes	
Energy	70 Kcal/293 kJ
Total fat	2.5 g
Saturated fat	0.4 g
Cholesterol	0 mg
Fibre	2.4 g

Drain the pasta, add it to the pan
sauce and toss well. Serve
mediately, sprinkled with basil leaves
d shaved Parmesan, if using.

VARIATION: To give the sauce a
more intense flavour, soak 15 g/½ oz
dried porcini mushrooms in
175 ml/6 fl oz/¾ cup warm water
for 15–20 minutes, then drain, chop
and add with the meat.

Spaghetti with Lamb & Sweet Pepper Sauce

This simple but flavoursome sauce is a speciality of the Abruzzo-Molise region of Italy, to the east of Rome.

Serves 6

INGREDIENTS

15 ml/1 tbsp olive oil
250 g/9 oz boneless lean lamb neck
   fillet, diced
2 garlic cloves, finely chopped
2 bay leaves, torn
250 ml/8 fl oz/1 cup dry
   white wine
4 ripe Italian plum tomatoes, peeled
   and chopped
2 large red peppers, seeded and diced
450 g/1 lb dried spaghetti
salt and freshly ground
   black pepper

2 Sprinkle in the garlic and add the bay leaves, then pour in the wine and let it bubble until reduced.

3 Add the tomatoes and peppers ar stir to mix. Season again. Cover, brin to the boil, then reduce the heat and simmer gently for 45–55 minutes, or until the lamb is very tender. Stir occasionally during the cooking process and add a little water if the sauce becomes too dry.

1 Heat the oil in a medium frying pan or saucepan, and add the lamb and a little salt and pepper. Cook over a medium to high heat for about 10 minutes, stirring frequently, until browned all over.

Meanwhile, cook the pasta in a large saucepan of lightly salted boiling water until it is *al dente*. Drain well. Remove and discard the bay leaves from the lamb sauce before serving it with the cooked pasta.

Nutritional Notes	
Energy	179 Kcal/755 kJ
Total fat	5.0 g
Saturated fat	1.8 g
Cholesterol	28 mg
Fibre	1.4 g

Tagliatelle with Meat Sauce

This recipe is an authentic meat sauce – *ragù* – from the city of Bologna in Emilia-Romagna.

Serves 8

INGREDIENTS
450 g/1 lb dried tagliatelle
salt and freshly ground black pepper
freshly grated Parmesan cheese,
   to serve (optional)

FOR THE MEAT SAUCE
15 ml/1 tbsp olive oil
1 onion, finely chopped
2 carrots, finely chopped
2 celery sticks, finely chopped
2 garlic cloves, finely chopped
115 g/4 oz lean back bacon, diced
250 g/9 oz extra-lean
   minced beef
250 g/9 oz extra-lean
   minced pork
120 ml/4 fl oz/½ cup dry
   white wine
2 x 400 g/14 oz cans crushed Italian
   plum tomatoes
475–750 ml/16 fl oz–1¼ pints/2–3 cups
   beef stock

Nutritional Notes	
Energy	185 Kcal/782 kJ
Total fat	5.0 g
Saturated fat	1.7 g
Cholesterol	36.3 mg
Fibre	1.8 g

1 Make the meat sauce. Heat the oil in a large frying pan or saucepan. Add the vegetables, garlic and bacon and cook over a medium heat, stirring frequently, for 10 minutes, or until the vegetables have softened.

2 Add the minced beef and pork, reduce the heat and cook gently for 10 minutes, stirring frequently and breaking up any lumps in the meat with a wooden spoon.

3 Stir in salt and pepper to taste, then add the wine and stir again. Simmer for about 5 minutes, or until reduced.

4 Add the tomatoes and 250 ml/ 8 fl oz/1 cup of the stock and bring to the boil. Stir well, then reduce the heat. Half cover the pan with a lid and leave to simmer very gently for 2 hours. Stir occasionally and add more stock as it becomes absorbed.

Simmer the sauce, without a lid, a further 30 minutes, stirring quently. Meanwhile, cook the pasta a large saucepan of lightly salted iling water until it is *al dente*. Taste sauce and adjust the seasoning.

6 Drain the cooked pasta well and tip it into a warmed serving bowl. Pour the meat sauce over the pasta and toss well to combine. Serve immediately, sprinkled with the grated Parmesan, if using.

Spaghetti with Meatballs

Italian-style meatballs simmered in a sweet and spicy tomato sauce are truly delicious served with spaghetti.

Serves 8

INGREDIENTS
350 g/12 oz extra-lean minced beef
1 egg
60 ml/4 tbsp roughly chopped fresh flat
    leaf parsley
2.5 ml/½ tsp crushed dried red chillies
1 thick slice of white bread,
    crusts removed
30 ml/2 tbsp semi-skimmed milk
15 ml/1 tbsp olive oil
300 ml/½ pint/1¼ cups passata
400 ml/14 fl oz/1⅔ cups
    vegetable stock
5 ml/1 tsp sugar
450 g/1 lb dried spaghetti
salt and freshly ground
    black pepper
40 g/1½ oz freshly grated Parmesan
    cheese, to serve

1 Put the minced beef in a bowl. Add the egg, half the parsley and half the chillies. Season with plenty of salt and pepper. Mix well.

Nutritional Notes	
Energy	148 Kcal/622 kJ
Total fat	5.0 g
Saturated fat	1.9 g
Cholesterol	44.8 mg
Fibre	0.9 g

2 Tear the bread into small pieces and place in a small bowl. Moisten with the milk. Leave to soak for a few minutes, then squeeze out and discard the excess milk and crumble the bread over the meat mixture.

3 Mix everything together with a wooden spoon, then use your hands to squeeze and knead the mixture so that it becomes smooth and quite sticky.

4 Rinse your hands under the cold tap, then immediately pick up small pieces of the mixture and roll the meat between your palms to make 40–60 small balls. Place the meatballs on a tray and chill them in the fridge for about 30 minutes.

5 Heat the oil in a large non-stick frying pan. Cook the meatballs in batches until they are browned all over. Set them aside.

Pour the passata and stock into a large saucepan. Heat gently, then add the remaining chillies and the sugar, with salt and pepper to taste. Add the meatballs to the passata mixture, then bring to the boil. Reduce the heat, cover and simmer for 20 minutes, stirring occasionally.

7 Cook the pasta in a large saucepan of lightly salted boiling water until it is *al dente*. Drain well and tip it into a warmed large bowl. Pour the sauce over the pasta and toss gently to mix. Sprinkle with the remaining parsley and serve with grated Parmesan handed separately.

Lasagne

This is a delicious low-fat version of the classic Italian lasagne, ideal served with a mixed salad and crusty bread.

Serves 8

INGREDIENTS
1 large onion, chopped
2 garlic cloves, crushed
500 g/1¼ lb extra-lean minced beef
  or turkey
450 g/1 lb passata
5 ml/1 tsp dried mixed herbs
225 g/8 oz frozen leaf spinach, thawed
200 g/7 oz no-precook lasagne verdi
200 g/7 oz low-fat cottage cheese
mixed salad, to serve

FOR THE SAUCE
25 g/1 oz low-fat spread
25 g/1 oz plain flour
300 ml/½ pint/1¼ cups skimmed milk
1.5 ml/¼ tsp freshly ground nutmeg
25 g/1 oz freshly grated
  Parmesan cheese
salt and freshly ground black pepper

1 Put the onion, garlic and minced meat into a non-stick saucepan. Cook the mixture quickly for 5 minutes, stirring with a wooden spoon to separate the pieces, until the meat is lightly browned all over.

2 Add the passata, mixed herbs and seasoning and stir to combine. Bring to the boil, cover, then reduce the heat and allow to simmer for about 30 minutes, stirring occasionally.

3 Make the sauce. Put all the sauce ingredients, except the Parmesan cheese, into a saucepan. Cook until the sauce thickens, whisking constantly until bubbling and smooth. Turn the heat off. Adjust the seasoning to taste, add the Parmesan cheese to the sauce and stir to mix.

4 Preheat the oven to 190°C/375°F/ Gas 5. Lay the spinach leaves out on sheets of absorbent kitchen paper and pat them until they are dry.

5 Layer the meat mixture, lasagne, cottage cheese and spinach leaves in a 2 litre/3½ pint/8 cup ovenproof dish, starting and ending with the meat.

Nutritional Notes	
Energy	244 Kcal/1032 kJ
Total fat	4.8 g
Saturated fat	1.9 g
Cholesterol	37.9 mg
Fibre	2.0 g

6 Spoon the cheese sauce over the top of the layers to cover the meat completely and bake in the oven for 40–50 minutes, or until the cheese sauce is bubbling. Serve immediately with a mixed salad.

Tagliatelle with Broccoli & Spinach

This is an excellent Italian vegetarian supper dish. It is nutritious, filling and low-fat and needs no accompaniment.

Serves 4

INGREDIENTS
2 heads of broccoli
450 g/1 lb fresh spinach,
   stalks removed
freshly grated nutmeg
350 g/12 oz dried egg tagliatelle
15 ml/1 tbsp extra virgin olive oil
juice of ½ lemon
salt and freshly ground black pepper
15 g/½ oz freshly grated Parmesan cheese,
   to serve

1 Put the broccoli in the basket of a steamer, then cover and steam over a saucepan of boiling water for 10 minutes. Add the prepared spinach to the broccoli in the steamer, cover and steam for 4–5 minutes, or until both vegetables are tender.

Nutritional Notes	
Energy	288 Kcal/1218 kJ
Total fat	4.9 g
Saturated fat	1.0 g
Cholesterol	1.9 mg
Fibre	4.5 g

2 Towards the end of the cooking time, sprinkle the vegetables with nutmeg and salt and pepper to taste. Transfer the vegetables to a colander.

3 Add salt to the vegetable water in the steamer saucepan. Fill this pan with boiling water, then add the pasta and cook until it is *al dente*. Meanwhile, chop the broccoli and spinach on a board.

VARIATION: If you like, add a sprinkling of crushed dried chillies with the pepper in Step 2.

4 Drain the pasta. Heat the oil in the pasta pan, add the pasta and chopped vegetables and toss over a medium heat until evenly mixed. Sprinkle in the lemon juice and plenty of black pepper, then taste and add more lemon juice, salt and nutmeg if you like. Serve immediately, sprinkled with grated Parmesan and pepper.

Pasta with Pesto Sauce

Traditionally made with lashings of olive oil, this simple pesto sauce is still full of flavour but relatively low in fat.

Serves 4

INGREDIENTS
225 g/8 oz/2 cups dried fusilli
50 g/2 oz/1 cup fresh basil leaves
25 g/1 oz/½ cup parsley sprigs
1 garlic clove, crushed
25 g/1 oz/¼ cup pine nuts
115 g/4 oz/½ cup curd cheese
30 ml/2 tbsp freshly grated
    Parmesan cheese
salt and freshly ground black pepper

2 Meanwhile, put half the basil leaves and half the parsley, together with the crushed garlic, pine nuts and curd cheese into the bowl of a food processor or blender and process until the mixture is smooth.

1 Cook the pasta in a large saucepan of lightly salted boiling water until it is *al dente*. Drain well.

3 Add most of the remaining basil leaves and the rest of the parsley to the food processor, together with the grated Parmesan cheese and the salt and pepper. Process the mixture again until the herbs are finely chopped.

Nutritional Notes	
Energy	315 Kcal/1310 kJ
Total fat	10.2 g
Saturated fat	3.6 g
Cholesterol	4.0 mg
Fibre	2.23 g

4 Toss the pasta with pesto and serve on warmed plates. Garnish with fresh basil leaves.

VARIATION: You can use any chunky pasta shapes for this recipe. Farfalle, orecchiette and rotelle would all work well.

45

Pasta with Tomato & Chilli Sauce

In Italian this dish is called *pasta all'arrabbiata*, meaning rabid or angry, and describes the heat that comes from the chilli. Sugocasa is sieved tomatoes

Serves 4

INGREDIENTS

500 g/1¼ lb sugocasa
2 garlic cloves, crushed
150 ml/¼ pint/⅔ cups dry white wine
15 ml/1 tbsp sun-dried tomato purée
1 fresh red chilli
300 g/11 oz/generous 2½ cups dried penne
   or tortiglioni
60 ml/4 tbsp finely chopped fresh
   flat leaf parsley
salt and freshly ground black pepper
15 g/½ oz freshly grated Pecorino cheese,
   to serve

2 Remove the whole chilli from th
sauce and add half the chopped
parsley. Season to taste with salt and
freshly ground black pepper.

3 Drain the pasta and tip it into a
warmed serving bowl. Pour the sauc
over the pasta and toss to mix. Serve
once, sprinkled with a little grated
Pecorino and the remaining parsley.

1 Put the sugocasa, garlic, wine,
tomato purée and whole chilli in a
saucepan and bring to the boil. Cover,
reduce the heat and simmer gently,
stirring occasionally. Cook the pasta
in a large saucepan of lightly salted
boiling water until it is *al dente*.

Nutritional Notes	
Energy	287 Kcal/1220 kJ
Total fat	2.1 g
Saturated fat	0.7 g
Cholesterol	2.2 mg
Fibre	3.0 g

COOK'S TIP: If you prefer a hotte
flavour, finely chop the chilli after
removing it in Step 2 and return it
to the sauce.

Chifferi Rigati with Aubergine Sauce

Full of flavour, this excellent Italian vegetarian sauce goes well with any short pasta shape to create an appetizing lunch or supper dish.

Serves 6

INGREDIENTS
30 ml/2 tbsp olive oil
1 small fresh red chilli
2 garlic cloves
2 handfuls of fresh flat leaf parsley,
   roughly chopped, plus extra to garnish
450 g/1 lb aubergines,
   roughly chopped
1 handful of fresh basil leaves
200 ml/7 fl oz/scant 1 cup water
1 vegetable stock cube
8 ripe Italian plum tomatoes, peeled and
   finely chopped
60 ml/4 tbsp red wine
5 ml/1 tsp sugar
1 sachet saffron powder
2.5 ml/½ tsp paprika
450 g/1 lb/scant 4 cups dried short pasta,
   such as chifferi, rigati or penne
salt and freshly ground
   black pepper

1 Heat the oil in a large frying pan or saucepan and add the chilli, garlic cloves and half the parsley. Crush the garlic cloves with a wooden spoon to release their juices, then cover the pan and allow to cook over a low to medium heat for about 10 minutes, stirring occasionally.

2 Remove and discard the chilli. Add the aubergines to the pan with the remaining parsley and the basil. Pour in half the water. Crumble in the stock cube and stir until it has dissolved, then cover and cook, stirring frequently, for about 10 minutes.

3 Add the tomatoes, wine, sugar, saffron and paprika and season with salt and pepper to taste, then pour in the remaining water. Stir well, then replace the lid and cook for a further 30–40 minutes, stirring occasionally. Adjust the seasoning to taste.

Nutritional Notes	
Energy	300 Kcal/1274 kJ
Total fat	3.6 g
Saturated fat	0.6 g
Cholesterol	0 mg
Fibre	4.1 g

Meanwhile, cook the pasta in a
ge saucepan of lightly salted boiling
ter until it is *al dente*. Drain.

5 Add the aubergine sauce to the
cooked pasta, toss together to ensure
it is thoroughly mixed and serve
immediately, garnished with parsley.

Penne with Artichokes

This pasta sauce is garlicky and richly flavoured, perfect for a delicious light lunch or supper.

Serves 6

INGREDIENTS
juice of 1 lemon
2 globe artichokes
15 ml/1 tbsp olive oil
1 small fennel bulb, thinly sliced, with
    feathery tops reserved
1 onion, finely chopped
4 garlic cloves, finely chopped
1 handful of fresh flat leaf parsley,
    roughly chopped
400 g/14 oz can chopped Italian
    plum tomatoes
150 ml/¼ pint/⅔ cup dry
    white wine
350 g/12 oz/3 cups dried penne
10 ml/2 tsp capers, chopped
salt and freshly ground
    black pepper

1 Have ready a bowl of cold water to which you have added half the lemon juice. Cut off the artichokes stalks, then discard the outer leaves until the pale inner leaves at the base remain.

2 Cut off the tops of these leaves so that the base remains. Cut the base in half lengthways, then prise the hairy choke out of the centre with the tip of the knife and discard. Cut the artichokes lengthways into 5 mm/¼ in slices, adding them immediately to the bowl of water.

3 Bring a large saucepan of water to the boil. Add a pinch of salt, and then drain the artichokes and add them immediately to the water. Boil for 5 minutes, drain and set aside.

4 Heat the oil in a large frying pan or saucepan and add the fennel, onion garlic and parsley. Cook over a low to medium heat, stirring frequently, for about 10 minutes, until the fennel has softened and is lightly coloured.

5 Add the tomatoes and wine, with salt and freshly ground black pepper taste. Bring to the boil, stirring, then cover, reduce the heat and simmer fo 10–15 minutes, stirring occasionally. Stir in the sliced artichokes, replace the lid and simmer for a further 10 minutes.

6 Meanwhile, cook the pasta in a large saucepan of lightly salted boiling water until it is *al dente*. Drain, reservi a little cooking water.

Stir the capers into the sauce, then just the seasoning if necessary and d the remaining lemon juice.

Tip the pasta into a warmed bowl, ur the sauce over and mix, adding a tle cooking water if necessary. Serve, rnished with fennel fronds.

Nutritional Notes	
Energy	269 Kcal/1140 kJ
Total fat	3.0 g
Saturated fat	0.4 g
Cholesterol	0 mg
Fibre	2.7 g

Penne with Green Vegetable Sauce

Lightly cooked fresh green vegetables are tossed with pasta to create this low-fat Italian dish, ideal for a light lunch or supper.

Serves 4

INGREDIENTS
2 carrots
1 courgette
75 g/3 oz French beans
1 small leek, washed
2 ripe Italian plum tomatoes
1 handful of fresh flat
    leaf parsley
15 ml/1 tbsp extra virgin olive oil
2.5 ml/½ tsp sugar
115 g/4 oz/1 cup frozen peas
350 g/12 oz/3 cups dried penne
salt and freshly ground
    black pepper

1 Dice the carrots and the courgette finely. Top and tail the French beans, then cut them into 2 cm/¾ in lengths. Slice the leek thinly. Peel and dice the plum tomatoes. Finely chop the flat leaf parsley and set it aside until it is needed.

2 Heat the oil in a medium frying pan or saucepan. Add the carrots and leek. Sprinkle in the sugar and cook, stirring frequently, for about 5 minutes.

3 Stir in the courgette, French beans, peas and salt and pepper to taste. Cover and cook over a low to medium heat for 5–8 minutes, until the vegetables are tender, stirring occasionally.

4 Meanwhile, cook the pasta in a large saucepan of lightly salted boiling water until it is *al dente*. Drain the pasta well and keep it hot until the dish is ready to serve.

Nutritional Notes	
Energy	328 Kcal/1392 kJ
Total fat	4.5 g
Saturated fat	0.7 g
Cholesterol	0 mg
Fibre	5.0 g

5 Stir the parsley and chopped plum tomatoes into the vegetable mixture and adjust the seasoning to taste. Toss with the pasta and serve at once.

COOK'S TIP: Prepare the leek by cutting along it several times almost to the root, then slicing across it.

Herb Pasta Crescents

Spinach and cottage cheese make a melt-in-the-mouth filling for these tasty fresh pasta crescents.

Serves 4

INGREDIENTS
1 quantity of basic pasta dough, with
   45 ml/3 tbsp chopped fresh herbs added
egg white, beaten, for brushing
flour, for dusting
chopped parsley, to garnish

FOR THE FILLING
225 g/8 oz frozen chopped spinach
1 small onion, finely chopped
pinch of freshly grated nutmeg
115 g/4 oz low-fat cottage cheese
1 egg, beaten
25 g/1 oz freshly grated Parmesan cheese
Salt and freshly ground black pepper

FOR THE SAUCE
300 ml/½ pint/1¼ cups skimmed milk
25 g/1 oz sunflower margarine
45 ml/3 tbsp plain flour
1.5 ml/¼ tsp freshly grated nutmeg
30 ml/2 tbsp chopped fresh herbs (chives,
   basil and parsley)

1 To make the filling, put the spinach and onion into a pan, cover and cook slowly for 10 minutes to thaw. Remove the lid and increase the heat to drive off any water. Season with salt, pepper and nutmeg. Turn the mixture into a bowl and cool slightly. Stir in the cottage cheese, beaten egg and the grated Parmesan cheese.

2 Roll the herb pasta into sheets 3 mm/⅛ in thick. Cut into 7.5 cm/ 3 in rounds with a fluted pastry cutter.

3 Place a teaspoonful of filling in the centre of each round. Brush the edges with egg white. Fold each in half to make crescents. Press the edges together with a fork to seal. Transfer t a floured dish towel and rest for 1 hou

4 To make the sauce, put the milk, margarine and flour in a saucepan an whisk constantly over a medium heat until the mixture is thickened and smooth. Season to taste with nutmeg salt and freshly ground black pepper. Stir in the chopped fresh herbs.

Nutritional Notes	
Energy	421 Kcal/1768 kJ
Total fat	14 g
Saturated fat	3.8 g
Cholesterol	184 mg
Fibre	3.6 g

5 Cook the pasta crescents in a large saucepan of lightly salted boiling water in batches, for 2–3 minutes, until they are *al dente*. Drain thoroughly.

6 Put the crescents on to warmed serving plates and pour over the herb sauce. Garnish with parsley leaves and serve at once.

Prawn & Pasta Salad with Green Dressing

The superb combination of seafood and pasta is enhanced by a delicious piquant dressing.

Serves 4–6

INGREDIENTS
4 anchovy fillets, drained
60 ml/4 tbsp skimmed milk
225 g/8 oz squid
15 ml/1 tbsp chopped capers
15 ml/1 tbsp chopped gherkins
1–2 garlic cloves, crushed
150 ml/¼ pint/⅔ cup low-fat
   natural yogurt
30–45 ml/2–3 tbsp reduced-fat
   mayonnaise
dash of lemon juice
50 g/2 oz watercress,
   finely chopped
30 ml/2 tbsp chopped fresh parsley
30 ml/2 tbsp chopped fresh basil
350 g/12 oz dried fusilli
350 g/12 oz peeled prawns
salt and freshly ground
   black pepper

1 Put the anchovies into a small bowl and cover with the milk. Leave to soak for 10 minutes.

2 Pull the head from the body of each squid and remove the quill. Peel the outer speckled skin from the bodies. Cut the tentacles from the heads and rinse under cold water. Cut into 5 mm/¼ in rings.

3 To make the dressing, mix the capers, gherkins, garlic, yogurt, mayonnaise, lemon juice, watercress and fresh herbs in a bowl. Drain and chop the anchovies. Add to the dressing and season to taste.

4 Drop the squid into a large pan of lightly salted boiling water. Lower the heat and simmer for 1–2 minutes.

5 Remove the squid rings and tentacles from the water with a slotted spoon. Cook the pasta in the same water until it is *al dente*. Drain well.

6 Mix the prawns and squid into the dressing in a large bowl. Add the pasta, toss and serve warm or cold as a salad.

Nutritional Notes	
Energy	502 Kcal/2107 kJ
Total fat	6.9 g
Saturated fat	1.1 g
Cholesterol	72 mg
Fibre	3.2 g

Tuna Pasta Salad

Serves 4

INGREDIENTS
450 g/1 lb/scant 4 cups short pasta, such as
    ruote, macaroni or farfalle
30 ml/2 tbsp olive oil
325 g/11½ oz can tuna in brine, drained
    and flaked
500 g/1¼ lb canned cannellini or borlotti
    beans, rinsed and drained
1 small red onion, very thinly sliced
2 celery sticks, very thinly sliced
juice of 1 lemon
30 ml/2 tbsp chopped fresh parsley
salt and freshly ground black pepper

1   Cook the pasta in a large saucepan
of lightly salted boiling water until it is
al dente. Drain, rinse under cold water.
Drain again and turn into a bowl. Toss
with olive oil and allow to cool.

2   Mix the tuna, beans, onion and
celery into the pasta. Combine the
lemon juice and parsley and pour over.
Season, and serve after 1 hour.

Nutritional Notes	
Energy	275 Kcal/1145 kJ
Total fat	7.4 g
Saturated fat	0.9 g
Cholesterol	41.3 mg
Fibre	0 g

*Right: Tuna Pasta Salad (top); Chicken
Pasta Salad*

Chicken Pasta Salad

Serves 4

INGREDIENTS
350 g/12 oz/3 cups short pasta, such as
    mezze rigatoni, fusilli or penne
22.5 ml/4½ tsp olive oil
225 g/8 oz/1½ cups cooked chicken
2 small red and yellow peppers
    (about 200 g/7 oz)
50 g/2 oz/⅓ cup stoned green olives
4 spring onions, chopped
45 ml/3 tbsp low-fat natural yogurt
15 ml/1 tbsp wine vinegar
salt and freshly ground
    black pepper

1   Cook the pasta in a large saucepan
of lightly salted boiling water until it is
al dente. Drain, rinse under cold water.
Drain again and turn into a bowl. Toss
with olive oil and allow to cool.

2   Cut the chicken into bite-size
pieces. Cut the peppers into small
pieces. Combine all the ingredients,
except the pasta, in a bowl. Taste for
seasoning, then mix into the pasta.
Serve chilled.

Nutritional Notes	
Energy	466 Kcal/1938 kJ
Total fat	9.6 g
Saturated fat	1.89 g
Cholesterol	46.6 mg
Fibre	0 g

Duck Breast Salad

Succulent duck breasts are first grilled, then sliced and tossed together with pasta and fresh fruit in a delicious, virtually fat-free dressing to create this tempting and colourful salad.

Serves 6

INGREDIENTS

2 duck breasts, boned
5 ml/1 tsp coriander seeds, crushed
350 g/12 oz/3 cups dried rigatoni
150 ml/¼ pint/⅔ cup fresh
    orange juice
15 ml/1 tbsp lemon juice
10 ml/2 tsp clear honey
1 shallot, finely chopped
1 garlic clove, crushed
1 celery stick, chopped
75 g/3 oz dried cherries
45 ml/3 tbsp port or red wine
15 ml/1 tbsp chopped fresh mint, plus
    extra to garnish
30 ml/2 tbsp chopped fresh coriander, plus
    extra to garnish
1 eating apple, cored and diced
2 oranges, segmented
salt and freshly ground
    black pepper

1 Remove and discard the skin and fat from the duck breasts and season with salt and freshly ground black pepper. Rub the duck breasts all over with crushed coriander seeds.

2 Preheat the grill, then grill the duck for 7–10 minutes, depending on size. Wrap in foil and set aside for about 20 minutes.

3 Meanwhile, cook the pasta in a large saucepan of lightly salted boiling water until it is *al dente*. Drain and rinse under cold running water, then drain again. Leave to cool.

4 Meanwhile, make the dressing. Put the orange juice, lemon juice, honey, shallot, garlic, celery, dried cherries, port or red wine, chopped mint and coriander into a bowl. Whisk all the ingredients together, then set the dressing aside for 20–30 minutes.

5 Using a long, sharp knife, slice the duck very thinly. (It should be pink in the centre.)

Nutritional Notes	
Energy	298 Kcal/1266 kJ
Total fat	2.3 g
Saturated fat	0.5 g
Cholesterol	27.5 mg
Fibre	3 g

6 Put the pasta into a bowl, add the duck, dressing, diced apple and segments of orange. Toss well to mix. Transfer the salad to a serving plate and garnish with the extra mint and coriander. Serve.

Sweet & Sour Peppers with Bows

Brightly coloured peppers combine with pasta and fresh coriander to add delicious flavour to this quick and easy warm salad.

Serves 8

INGREDIENTS
1 red, 1 yellow and 1 orange pepper
1 garlic clove, crushed
30 ml/2 tbsp capers
30 ml/2 tbsp raisins
5 ml/1 tsp wholegrain mustard
finely grated rind and juice
    of 1 lime
5 ml/1 tsp clear honey
30 ml/2 tbsp chopped fresh coriander
225 g/8 oz/2 cups dried farfalle
salt and freshly ground black pepper
shaved Parmesan cheese,
    to serve (optional)

1 Quarter the peppers and remove and discard the stalks and seeds. Put into a saucepan of boiling water and cook for 10–15 minutes, until tender. Drain and rinse the peppers under cold water. Drain again. Peel away and discard the skin and cut the flesh into strips lengthways. Set aside.

2 Put the garlic, capers, raisins, mustard, lime rind and juice, honey, coriander and seasoning into a bowl and whisk together. Set aside.

3 Cook the pasta in a large saucepan of lightly salted boiling water until it *al dente*. Drain.

Nutritional Notes	
Energy	160 Kcal/681 kJ
Total fat	1.0 g
Saturated fat	0.2 g
Cholesterol	0 mg
Fibre	1.9 g

VARIATION: If you prefer, make this salad with only one colour of pepper. The green ones are too bitter, however, and are not suitable

4 Return the pasta to the pan, add the reserved peppers and dressing. Heat gently and toss to mix. Transfer to a serving bowl and serve warm, sprinkled with a few shavings of Parmesan cheese, if using.

This edition is published by Hermes House

Hermes House is an imprint of Anness Publishing Ltd
Hermes House, 88–89 Blackfriars Road, London SE1 8HA
tel. 020 7401 2077; fax 020 7633 9499; info@anness.com

© Anness Publishing Ltd 2000, 2004

Publisher: Joanna Lorenz
Editor: Valerie Ferguson
Series Designer: Bobbie Colgate Stone
Designer: Andrew Heath
Production Controller: Joanna King

Recipes contributed by: Catherine Atkinson, Angela Boggiano, Carla Capalbo,
Sue Maggs, Anne Sheasby, Jeni Wright.

Photography: William Adams-Lingwood, James Duncan, Amanda Heywood,
Janine Hosegood, Peter Reilly.

Previously published as *Low-Fat Pasta*

1 3 5 7 9 10 8 6 4 2

Notes:
For all recipes, quantities are given in both metric and imperial measures and, where appropriate measures are also given in standard cups and spoons.
Follow one set, but not a mixture, because they are not interchangeable.

Standard spoon and cup measures are level.

1 tsp = 5 ml   1 tbsp = 15 ml

1 cup = 250 ml/8 fl oz

Australian standard tablespoons are 20 ml.
Australian readers should use 3 tsp in place of
1 tbsp for measuring small quantities of gelatine, cornflour, salt etc.

Medium eggs are used unless otherwise stated.